EARTH CYCLES

EARTH'S ENERGY SOURCES

by Sally Morgan

A+

Smart Apple Media

Published by Smart Apple Media
P.O. Box 3263, Mankato, Minnesota 56002

Printed in the United States of America at Corporate Graphics, in North Mankato, Minnesota.

Published by arrangement with the Watts Publishing Group Ltd., London.

Library of Congress Cataloging-in-Publication Data
Morgan, Sally, 1957-
  Earth's Energy Sources / by Sally Morgan.
      p. cm. -- (Earth cycles)
  Includes bibliographical references and index.
  Summary: "Presents the many ways we harness light, food, wind, and fossil fuels and how we use that energy. Discusses the harmful effects fossil fuels have on our environment and suggests ways for readers to help conserve energy. Includes diagrams"--Provided by publisher.
  ISBN 978-1-59920-522-9 (library binding : alk. paper)
 1. Power resources--Juvenile literature. 2. Energy conservation--Juvenile literature. 3. Recycling (Waste, etc.)--Juvenile literature. I. Title.
  TJ163.23.M668 2012
  333.79--dc22

                                   2010030439

Produced for Franklin Watts by
White-Thomson Publishing, Ltd.
Editor: Jean Coppendale
Design: Paul Manning

Picture credits
t = top b = bottom l = left = r = right
Cover main, 1: ECO/Jon Bower; cover t: ECO/Matthew Bolton; cover middle: Shutterstock/Robert Ladkowski; cover b, 18t: Shutterstock/Ivars Linards Zolnerovics; 3l, 6b: Shutterstock/Leah-Anne Thompson; 3r, 20b: Wikipedia/USAF; 4b: Shutterstock/Alexia Khruscheva; 4t: ECO/Phillip Colla; 5l: ECO/Fritz Polking; 5r: Shutterstock/Sebastian Kaulitzki; 6r: Shutterstock/AMA; 7l: Shutterstock/Digital Sport Photo Agency; 7r, 30: Shutterstock/Suzanne Tucker; 8: Shutterstock/T. Kachuk; 8: Stefan Chabluk; 9l: ECO/Peter Landon; 9r: ECO/Peter Currell; 10: Shutterstock/Andresr/Paul Cowan; 11l: Shutterstock/Jakub Cejpek; 11b: Shutterstock/M@verick Maverick; 11r: Shutterstock/Val Thoermer; 12 : Shutterstock/Johan Swanepoel; 12: Stefan Chabluk; 13: ECO/Phillip Colla; 14b: ECO/Chinch Gryniewicz; 14t: ECO/Peter Hulme; 14r: ECO/John Liddiard; 14b: ECO/Chinch Gryniewicz; 15l: Peter Menzel/Science Photo Library; 15r: Ecoscene/Frank Blackburn; 16b: ECO/Barry Webb; 16t: Shutterstock/Robert Ladkowski; 17l: Shutterstock/Yvan; 17r: ECO/Peter Currell; 18b: ECO/Chris Knapton; 19l: Shutterstock/Ian Bracegirdle; 19r: Shutterstock/Iofoto; 20t: Shutterstock/ Markus Gann; 21l: GNU/Hans Hillewaert (Lycaon); 21r: ECO/Chinch Gryniewicz; 22b: Shutterstock/Ulrich Mueller; 22t: ECO/Tony Page; 23b: Shutterstock/Olexa; 23m: ECO/David Wootton Photography; 23r: Shutterstock/Restyler; 24: Shutterstock/Bart Everett; : 24t: Paul Manning; 25r: ECO/Angela Hampton; 26: Shutterstock/Sandra Kemppainen; 27r: ECO/Chinch Gryniewicz; 27l: Shutterstock/Vera Bogaerts; 28l: ECO/Angela Hampton; 28b: ECO/Peter Cairns; 28r: Shutterstock/Kelpfish; 29l: Shutterstock/Karin Lau; 29r: ECO/Sally Morgan.

Note to parents and teachers
Every effort has been made by the publishers to ensure that the web sites listed on page 32 are suitable for children, that they are of the highest educational value, and that they contain no inappropriate or offensive material. However, because of the nature of the Internet, it is impossible to guarantee that the contents of these sites have not been altered. We strongly advise that Internet access is supervised by a responsible adult.

1018
3-2011

9 8 7 6 5 4 3 2 1

Contents

Words appearing in **bold** like this can be found in the glossary on pages 30–31.

What Is Energy?

All life needs energy. Plants and animals, including people, need it to grow and to **reproduce**. People also need energy to heat their homes, to cook food, and to power machines.

Spending Energy

You cannot see energy. It is not a substance such as water, so you cannot touch it. Energy is the ability to do work. When you lift your arm, your muscles have to work and they use energy to do so. You can think of energy as money. You need money to be able to buy something. Energy is similar, for in order to do work you need to spend some energy.

▲ At night, a vast amount of electrical energy is used to light up our cities.

► A running horse uses a lot of energy to move its legs.

The Sun

The source of most of the earth's energy is the sun. It heats the **atmosphere** and provides light energy for plants so they can make food. This food is eaten by animals that need energy to move around. Plants and animals also need water. The water on earth is recycled over and over again, forming a **water cycle**. Unlike water however, energy is not recycled. Instead, energy from the sun is used by plants and other living things, and then it reenters space, usually as heat.

Q How much energy does the sun release in a second?

A A vast amount so large that it is difficult to imagine just how much. Just one second's worth of energy from the sun could provide the United States with energy for the next 9 million years.

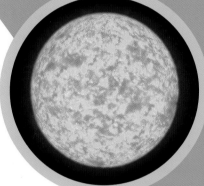

► In one second, the sun releases the equivalent of the annual energy of about 2 billion power plants.

▲ Water flowing down this waterfall has kinetic energy.

Energy Forms

There are many different forms of energy. **Kinetic energy** is energy that an object has because it is moving. **Potential energy** is the energy that an object has when it changes position. For example, if you hold an object high off the ground it has energy once it is dropped. **Stored energy** is potential energy too, such as the energy stored in food, in batteries, and in fuels such as oil, gas, and coal.

Energy Changes

One of the most important laws in science states that energy cannot be made or destroyed, but it can be changed from one form to another.

Electrical Energy

Electrical energy is a very common and useful form of energy. When you flip a light switch, electricity flows into the lightbulb where it is converted (changed) to light energy. When you listen to music on an iPod, electrical energy is changed into sound energy.

Potential Energy

Batteries are useful energy stores. When energy is needed, the potential energy locked up in the chemicals inside the battery is converted to electrical energy and used to power laptops and other equipment.

▼ This wind **turbine** converts kinetic energy to electrical energy.

▶ When this iPod is turned on, potential energy is changed to electrical energy, which is then changed to sound energy.

Wasted Energy

When energy is changed from one form to another, there is some waste, or unused energy. For example, when a lightbulb is switched on, some of the electrical energy is changed to useful light, but some is converted to heat. This is waste energy because the heat has no use. Fuel is burned in car engines to release energy that turns the wheels, but as much as two-thirds of the energy is changed to heat energy that escapes into the environment. The hot gases that escape out of the car's **exhaust** are wasted energy. The **efficiency** of an energy change tells us how much energy is wasted.

Q Is a bicycle more energy efficient than a car?

A Yes. Almost all the energy (about 95 percent) used by the cyclist to turn the pedals is converted into kinetic energy that spins the wheels. A car is only about 30 percent energy efficient.

▲ Bicycles are very efficient machines.

◀ Engines of racing cars produce a lot of waste heat. This is carried away through pipes to stop the engine from overheating.

Light Energy and Plants

Plants trap light energy from the sun and use it to make their food.

Trapping Light

Plants have green leaves because they contain a green **pigment** called **chlorophyll**. This pigment is essential to **photosynthesis**, the food-making process in plants. Chlorophyll traps light energy, which is used to combine **carbon dioxide** from the air and water from the ground to make food such as sugar and **starch**. **Oxygen** is produced in photosynthesis and most of it enters the atmosphere where it is used by animals in **respiration**.

▼ When plants photosynthesize during the day, they take carbon dioxide from the air and release oxygen back into the air.

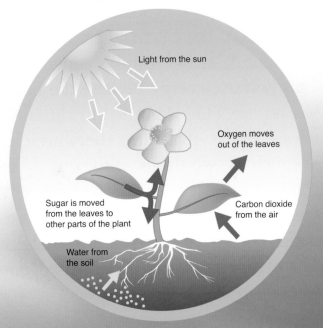

Light from the sun

Oxygen moves out of the leaves

Sugar is moved from the leaves to other parts of the plant

Carbon dioxide from the air

Water from the soil

▼ The sugars produced during photosynthesis are used by the sunflower plant to make flowers.

Q and A

Rich in Carbon

Carbon is an **element** like **hydrogen** and oxygen, and it is found in all living things. Substances that are rich in carbon store a lot of energy such as sugar and starch. **Fats** and oils contain even more carbon, so they store even more energy.

▶ Carrot plants store starch in their roots, the part that we eat.

Q How much of the light energy landing on a leaf is used by a plant?

A Only a tiny amount. Most of the light is reflected away by the leaf. The most efficient plants use less than 4 percent of the light landing on their leaves, and most only absorb 1–3 percent of the light.

▲ Some light passes straight through the leaves of a plant.

Respiration

When animal and plant **cells** need energy, sugar is broken down in a process called respiration. This releases energy, which is used by the cells to make new substances. This process is almost the opposite of photosynthesis. In photosynthesis, the plant makes sugars from carbon dioxide and water, but in respiration, sugar is broken down using oxygen. Respiration releases energy which is needed by the plant and produces carbon dioxide and water.

9

Food Chains

People and other animals cannot make their own food, so they eat ready-made sources, such as plants and other animals, to get their energy.

Producers

A **food chain** shows how living organisms get their food. Plants are **producers**, so they are at the bottom of the food chain, and they are eaten by animals.

▼ In this food chain, energy is transferred from one living thing to the next.

1
Plants use light energy from the sun to make food.

2
Herbivores, such as this grasshopper, feed on plants.

3
Carnivores, such as this shrew, feed on herbivores, such as grasshoppers.

◄ Lions are at the top of their food chain and are very successful hunters.

Q and A

Energy Transfer

When an herbivore eats a plant, it gains the energy locked up in the plant. The energy is transferred again when the herbivore is eaten by a carnivore. The carnivore may then be eaten by another carnivore and the energy is passed on again. At each transfer, only about 10 percent of the energy is passed on, and the rest is lost. For example, losses may occur because an herbivore may not eat all the parts of the plant.

Q What are the longest food chains?

A Ocean food chains. The producers are tiny plants called plant **plankton**. These are eaten by zooplankton, which are tiny animals. The zooplankton are eaten by small fish, which are eaten by larger fish. Then the larger fish are eaten by **predators** such as dolphins or seals, which may be eaten by large sharks.

5
The top carnivore, such as this eagle, is not hunted by any other animal.

4
Large carnivores, such as snakes, feed on small carnivores.

 This seal feeds on fish, but it may be eaten by larger predators such as sharks and killer whales.

11

Energy from Food

Food contains a mix of **carbohydrates**, fats, and **proteins**. These are substances that are needed by our body, and they contain energy. **Minerals**, **vitamins**, and **fiber** are also found in food.

Energy Content

The energy content of food depends on how much carbohydrate, fat, and protein is present. This is measured in **calories**. Food labels show how much energy is locked up in a particular food. Fats contain about twice as much energy as the same **mass** of carbohydrate. Because fatty foods contain so much energy, only small amounts should be eaten.

cheese and milk supply fat and protein

fish is rich in protein

fruit and vegetables supply minerals and vitamins

pasta and bread contain starch

▶ We need to eat a mix of carbohydrates, fats, and proteins to stay healthy.

chicken and other meats are rich in protein

Too Much Energy

When we eat food, it is **digested** and taken in to our body. Then the energy is used to power our daily activities such as keeping the body working, moving around, and exercising. If we take in too much energy, the body builds up its stores of fat to be used in the future. If we continue to eat too much food, thick layers of fat build up and we become overweight. If we take in too little energy, the body uses up its energy stores and we start to lose weight.

Q How much energy does a person need each day?
A The average young woman needs about 1,940 calories a day to carry out normal activities, while a young man needs about 2,550 calories. As people get older they require less energy.

► Exercise is good for you. You use 0.75 calorie for every pound of your body weight to run a mile.

▲ There are far more overweight people today than 20 years ago. This is partly because people are eating far more fatty foods, such as french fries, and exercising less.

Making Fossil Fuels

Some plant and animal remains do not get broken down. Instead, they become covered with mud. Over millions of years, they turn into **fossil fuels** such as coal, oil, and gas.

Making Coal

Coal is formed from plants, especially trees, that become buried in muddy **swamps**. Over many millions of years, more layers of mud form and they press down on the plant matter. First, it is changed into peat, which contains fragments of plant material. The peat is then gradually changed into coal after many millions of years of being squashed.

▲ Peat forms in swampy places where there is a lot of water.

▼ The coal on this fire is darker and harder and contains more carbon than wood, so it releases far more heat.

▲ These blocks of peat have been dug from the ground and can be burned on a fire.

Oil and Natural Gas

Oil and natural gas form from the remains of **microscopic** plants and animals that live in water. When these organisms die, their remains drop to the seabed, where they are quickly buried under layers of mud. The immense weight of layers of mud pushing down on the remains causes them to become a liquid, known as **crude oil**. Natural gas forms, too.

Q What is oil shale?

A Oil shale is a rock that is rich in a substance called kerogen. Oil shale is dug from the ground, crushed, and heated to turn the kerogen into oil.

▲ This piece of oil shale can be crushed and heated to extract the oil.

▶ Crude oil from the ground is a thick, dark brown or black liquid.

Energy Rich

Fossil fuels are rich in carbon so they are excellent energy stores. When they burn, the oxygen in the air reacts with the carbon to form carbon dioxide, and heat is released. This heat can be put to many uses such as heating homes, cooking food, and making electricity in power plants.

Finding Coal, Oil, and Gas

Coal, oil, and gas are found in the ground in different parts of the world.

Coal Mining

Coal is a hard rock that is dug from the ground. The best coal is a black coal, which has the highest energy content. Brown coal is a younger coal and contains less energy. Sometimes the coal lies close to the earth's surface so it is easily reached by digging large holes in the ground. This is called **surface mining**. Coal that occurs deeper in the ground is reached by digging a **mine shaft** vertically through the ground. Then horizontal tunnels are dug from the shaft to mine the coal.

▲ Black coal burns more cleanly than brown coal, so it produces less air pollution.

▶ Huge machines dig out coal from this surface mine in Wales.

Q and A

Oil and Gas

Oil and gas are found underground in oil rocks, such as sandstone, shale, and limestone. These are rocks with lots of small holes filled with oil. Some oil is found under the land, but there is also oil under the seabed. Wells are sunk deep into the ground to pump out the oil and gas. Crude oil is a mix of substances, so it is sent to an **oil refinery** where they are all separated. The substances include gasoline, **diesel**, **aviation fuel**, and **bitumen**.

Q Why is natural gas given a smell?

A Natural gas has no smell. This means it could leak from pipes without people knowing. The gas could catch fire and cause an explosion. By adding a smell, any leaks can be detected and repaired.

▼ This North Sea oil platform is anchored to the seabed so that engineers can drill down through the seabed to reach the oil.

▲ Gas does not have a smell when it burns, but it does when it escapes from pipes.

Generating Electricity

Much of the world's electricity is produced in power plants that burn fossil fuels. The process of **generating** electricity involves changing kinetic energy into electrical energy.

Many different fuels can be used in power plants, including fossil fuels, **uranium**, and wood. **Renewable energy** sources can be used, too, such as running water, wind, and the sun.

▲ Coal is bulky, so it is usually transported from a mine to a power plant by train.

Turbines

Turbines are a key part of electricity generation. A turbine is a machine with blades that spin. In a fossil fuel power plant, the fuel is burned to release heat, which is used to heat up water and produce steam. A jet of steam is directed into the turbines where it spins the blades. The kinetic energy of the blades is changed into electrical energy in the generator.

turbine blades

► Turbine blades can be driven by wind, steam, or water. This turbine on a river is turned by water.

Q and A

Efficiency

Unfortunately, the process of generating electricity is not very efficient. Only a third or so of the energy locked up in the fuel is changed into electrical energy. In the future, better use may be made of the waste heat from the steam, which can be used for heating homes and factories near the power plant.

Q What is **nuclear energy**?

A This is energy that is released when the metal uranium is bombarded with tiny particles called **electrons**. This takes place in a nuclear power plant. About 16 percent of the world's electricity is generated using uranium as the fuel.

▼ A lot of the heat energy produced by a coal-fired power plant escapes into the atmosphere.

▲ This nuclear power plant in Florida supplies electricity to half a million homes.

Using the Sun, Wind, and Water

Fossil fuels are not the only source of energy. It is possible to capture energy directly from the sun, wind, and moving water. These renewable energy sources are becoming more important as fossils fuels start to run low.

Using Light

Heat from the sun can be trapped by **solar panels** placed in sunny places, such as on roofs. They take in heat from the sun and use it to warm water. Another type of panel, the **photovoltaic panel**, takes in sunlight and converts it directly into electricity.

▲ Solar panels are usually placed on south-facing roofs to get the maximum amount of light.

▼ There are many solar power plants in the southern United States where the **climate** is sunny for much of the year.

Water Power

Falling water has a lot of energy—the farther it falls, the more energy it has. Dams are built across rivers to create a **reservoir**, or lake, of water. The water is let out of the reservoir and it falls down a pipe in the dam to the turbines at the bottom where the electricity is generated.

Wind Power

Wind farms containing many turbines are a common sight in windy places such as mountains and along coastlines. A wind turbine uses the force of the wind to spin the blades. The electricity generated by the turbine is carried by cables to nearby towns and cities. Small wind turbines can be attached to buildings to generate electricity for lighting and for powering electrical equipment.

Q Can wave energy generate electricity?

A Yes. Floating wave machines can generate electricity by using the kinetic energy of waves. The energy of waves battering the coast can also be trapped by wave power plants on coastlines. As the waves rush into the power plant, the water forces air to enter the turbine, where its kinetic energy is changed into electrical energy.

◀ This wind farm has been built in shallow water off the coast of Belgium.

▲ Waves are a newly discovered source of renewable energy. They can be used to help generate electricity.

Biofuels

Biofuels are fuels made from plants, the producers in the food chain. The plants are **harvested** and burned to release heat.

▲ Some power plants use straw as fuel.

Burning Wood

Wood, charcoal, straw, and bamboo are all examples of biofuels. Plants contain carbon and when they burn, they release a lot of heat. Wood has been used by people to supply heat and for cooking for millions of years. Charcoal is produced by burning wood without any oxygen. This leaves lumps of pure carbon. Straw, another biofuel, is the dried stalks of cereal crops, such as wheat and barley, which are left behind after harvesting.

▼ These stocks of timber and wood pellets can be used to produce energy in a biofuel power plant.

Q and A

Q Can engines run on peanut oil?
A Yes, at the end of the 19th century, the inventor of the diesel engine, Karl Diesel, demonstrated his engine using a vegetable oil from peanuts as the fuel. It was only later that cars were powered by diesel fuel from crude oil.

Energy Crops

Some fast-growing plants such as willow, bamboo, and elephant grass are grown as energy crops. Within a year or so, the stems can be cut down and used as a fuel. The plant regrows and can be harvested again.

Oil Seeds

Many plants, such as **rapeseed, oil palm,** and sunflowers produce oil-rich seeds. The oil can be collected, refined, and used as **biodiesel** in cars and other vehicles.

▼ Seeds of the rapeseed plant are crushed to release oil.

▼ Some wheat is grown for fuel rather than for food.

▲ Many cars with diesel engines can run on fuel made from vegetable oil.

More Carbon Dioxide

When fossil fuels burn, they release carbon dioxide. Since the end of World War II (1939–45), the use of fossil fuels, especially oil and gas, has increased enormously and so has the level of carbon dioxide in the atmosphere.

▼ This diagram shows how heat from the earth's surface is trapped in the atmosphere by greenhouse gases.

Greenhouse Gas

Carbon dioxide is a **greenhouse gas**. This means that it traps heat in the atmosphere. Carbon dioxide is released when fossil fuels, biofuels, and even paper are burned because they all contain carbon. As more fuels are burned, more carbon dioxide is released and more heat is trapped.

Some energy is reflected back into space

Energy from the sun passes through the atmosphere to the earth's surface

Heat from the earth's surface radiates out to space

Heat trapped in the atmosphere by greenhouse gases

▼ Carbon dioxide is produced when oil is burned in the engines of cars and other vehicles.

Global Warming

The increase in carbon dioxide is slowly increasing the average temperature of the earth's surface. This is called **global warming**. Unfortunately, this is having a widespread effect on the earth's climates and thus on many different fragile environments, such as coral reefs and the Arctic. Climates are becoming less predictable, and extreme weather such as droughts, floods, and severe storms are more common.

Rising Seas

Sea levels are rising, too. This is caused by seawater becoming warmer and expanding. Also, **glaciers** and the polar **ice caps** are melting, and more water is pouring into the oceans. This is flooding low-lying islands and coastal regions.

Q Are there any other greenhouses gases?

A Yes, several gases are greenhouse gases. The list includes **methane, nitrous oxide, CFCs, ozone,** and even **water vapor.** Methane is released from rotting vegetation, swamps, and even cows! Nitrous oxide is released by bacteria in the soil, as well as by industry.

▲ About a quarter of the methane in the atmosphere comes from livestock such as cows when they digest their food.

25

Sustainable Energy

Sustainable is a word that is used a lot today. Sustainable energy is a source of energy that meets the needs of people today, while making sure that there is enough energy in the future.

It is important to use **resources** that can be renewed or replaced. For example, wood is a sustainable energy source because trees can be cut down and new trees can be planted in their place. Biofuels are sustainable because the crops that make them can be replanted.

▼ Fast-growing trees, such as conifers, are planted as a sustainable crop. The straight trunks provide timber and pulp for paper. They are cut down after about 30 years and replanted.

Carbon Dioxide In and Out

Biofuels are **carbon neutral**. This means when they are burned they produce carbon dioxide, just like fossil fuels. However, while they are growing, they take in carbon dioxide for photosynthesis. This means that during the cycle, from seed to fuel, the intake of carbon dioxide equals the release of carbon dioxide. Using biofuels therefore helps to combat global warming.

Q What is biogas?

A Biogas is a mix of gases including methane, which forms when materials such as waste food, sewage, or animal dung is broken down in an airtight container. Biogas can be used for heating, cooking, in industry, and even in cars.

▲ Some people are concerned that plants grown for biofuels, such as this elephant grass, take up land that could be used for food crops.

▲ Biogas is used in this kitchen in India.

Renewable Energy

Wind, solar, and water energy are often called renewable energy sources because their supply is never ending. They can be used continually as the supply will never run out. Although this energy is not easy to capture, it is clean, unlike fossil fuels.

Saving Energy

Every day, the world's population increases. This means there is an even greater demand for energy. Unfortunately, fossil fuels are not renewable, and they will run out. Everyone has to try to use less energy so that the remaining supplies last longer.

▼ Walking to school is good exercise and helps to save energy.

What Can You Do?

There are simple things to do at home that help save energy. It may not seem like much, but if everyone did a little it would help a lot. For example, turn off electrical equipment when not in use rather than leaving it on standby. Turn off lights when leaving a room, and use low-energy lightbulbs. Wear more clothes rather than turn up the heat.

▼ A low-energy bulb uses about one-fifth the energy and lasts 12 times as long as a traditional bulb.

▲ Turn down the heat to save energy.

Q and A

Traveling Around

Traveling uses a lot of energy. Each day, people travel in cars, buses, or trains to school or work. Many people fly to other parts of the world on business or to go on vacation. We can help by cutting down on unnecessary travel and choosing to walk, bike, or take public transportation whenever possible.

Low-Energy Cars

Some cars use less fuel than others, so they travel much farther on a gallon of gas. There are also electric cars that run on batteries rather than gas. These cars save energy and reduce the amount of carbon dioxide released into the atmosphere.

Q How does **insulating** our homes save energy?
A A lot of heat escapes from the walls, roofs, and windows of our homes. By laying thick insulation in the roof and installing double-pane windows, far less heat escapes. Less heat is needed to keep the home warm.

▲ About a quarter of the heat loss from a house occurs through an uninsulated roof.

▲ This car is powered by a battery. It does not use gas. Electricity is used to recharge the battery.

Glossary

atmosphere a layer of gases surrounding the earth

aviation fuel a type of oil used in the engines of airplanes

biodiesel a fuel made from plants such as rapeseed

biofuel a fuel made from plant matter

bitumen a sticky tar that is formed when oil is refined

calorie a unit of energy

carbohydrate an energy-rich substance such as starch and sugar

carbon dioxide a colorless gas found in the air

carbon neutral when the amount of carbon dioxide taken in by plants during their growth is the same as the amount that is released when they are burned

carnivore an animal that eats other animals

cell the basic unit of any living thing; some organisms consist of just one cell; most animals are made up of billions of cells.

CFCs harmful substances that were used in aerosols, refrigerators, and freezers but are now banned

chlorophyll the green substance found in plants

climate the regular pattern of weather experienced by a region or country

crude oil the thick black oil that comes from the ground

diesel a fuel produced from oil

digest to break down food that has been eaten in the stomach

efficiency comparison of energy output to energy input in a device such as an engine

electron a tiny particle that is part of an atom and has a negative charge

element a substance that cannot be broken down into different kinds of matter, for example carbon and oxygen

exhaust the part of the engine from which hot waste gases are released

fats one of the three main nutrients in food; fats are rich in stored energy.

fiber part of food that cannot be broken down but which helps the process of digestion

food chain the feeding relationships between a sequence of organisms

fossil fuel fuels made millions of years ago, including coal, oil, and natural gas

generate to produce; power plants generate electricity.

glacier a slow-moving mass of ice

global warming the warming of the surface of the earth due to an increase in greenhouse gases

greenhouse gas a gas that traps heat in the atmosphere

harvest to gather crops and other plants when they are ripe

herbivore a plant-eating animal

hydrogen an element; a type of gas

ice cap the thick mass of ice at the poles

insulate to use material to trap heat; to keep something warm

kinetic energy energy contained within an object that is moving

mass the amount of matter in an object, usually measured in pounds, grams, or kilograms

methane a greenhouse gas

microscopic not large enough to be seen by the naked eye but visible through a miscroscope

mineral a substance needed by the body in small amounts for healthy growth

mine shaft a vertical passageway from the surface to tunnels underground where coal is mined

nitrous oxide a greenhouse gas

nuclear energy electricity produced in a power plant that is fueled by uranium

oil palm a type of palm tree that produces fruits containing a lot of oil

oil refinery a place where crude oil is made into different products

oxygen a colorless gas found in air

ozone a colorless gas

photosynthesis the process by which plants make their food using light energy, carbon dioxide, and water

photovoltaic panel a solar panel that converts sunlight into electricity

pigment a substance that gives an object a color

plankton tiny plants and animals floating in the upper layers of the ocean

potential energy the energy stored in an object; this energy can be converted into other forms of energy.

predator an animal that hunts other animals

producer an organism that can make its own food, such as a plant

protein a nutrient found in food, used for growth and repair

rapeseed a plant related to cabbage that is grown for its oil

renewable energy energy that is obtained from sources, such as the sun and wind, that will not run out

reproduce to breed; to produce young

reservoir a large lake that forms behind a dam

resources things that can be used by people; raw materials

respiration the process that breaks down sugars and other substances to release energy

solar panels structures that trap light to heat water or produce electricity

starch an energy-rich substance made by plants

stored energy energy that is locked up in something, such as a battery

surface mining a type of mining which takes place on the earth's surface

swamp a wetland habitat

turbine a device that consists of blades that are spun by the force of moving water, wind, or steam; a turbine is often used in generating electricity.

uranium a metal used as a fuel in nuclear power stations

vitamin a substance needed in tiny amounts in the diet

water cycle the circulation of the earth's water from the sea into the atmosphere and back again

water vapor water that is in the form of a gas

Further Reading

Laidlaw, Jill. *Energy.* Amicus, 2011.

Morris, Neil. *The Energy Mix.* Smart Apple Media, 2010.

Oxlade, Chris and Terry Jennings. *Energy.* Smart Apple Media, 2009.

Web Sites

EERE: Kids Home Page: www.eere.energy.gov/kids/
Visit the U.S. Department of Energy's web site about how to save energy.

EIA - Energy Kids Energy Information Administration: www.eia.doe.gov/kids/energyfacts/
The U.S. Energy Information Administration site has facts and information about energy.

Geography4Kids.com: www.geography4kids.com/files/cycles_energy.html
Find information about the energy cycle and other geography topics.

Index